THE TUNDRA

DISCOVER THIS FROZEN BIOME

Philip Johansson

Enslow Elementary

an imprint of

Enslow Publishers, Inc.

40 Industrial Road
Box 398
Berkeley Heights, NJ 07922
USA

www.enslow.com

Enslow Elementary, an imprint of Enslow Publishers, Inc.
Enslow Elementary® is a registered trademark of Enslow Publishers, Inc.

Originally published as *The Frozen Tundra: A Web of Life* in 2004.

Library of Congress Cataloging-in-Publication Data

Johansson, Philip.
    The tundra : discover this frozen biome / Philip Johansson.
        pages cm. — (Discover the world's biomes)
    "Originally published as The frozen tundra: a web of life in 2004."
    Includes bibliographical references and index.
    ISBN 978-0-7660-6425-6
    1. Tundra ecology—Juvenile literature. I. Title. II. Series: Johansson, Philip. Discover the world's biomes.
    QH541.5.T8J63 2015
    577.5'86—dc23
                 2014027459

Summary: "Discusses the plants and animals of the tundra biome, including their roles in the food chain"—Provided by publisher.

Future editions:
Paperback ISBN: 978-0-7660-6426-3   EPUB ISBN: 978-0-7660-6427-0
Single-User PDF ISBN: 978-0-7660-6428-7   Multi-User PDF ISBN: 978-0-7660-6429-4

Printed in the United States of America
102014 Bang Printing, Brainerd, Minn.
10 9 8 7 6 5 4 3 2 1

To Our Readers: We have done our best to make sure all Internet addresses in this book were active and appropriate when we went to press. However, the author and the publisher have no control over and assume no liability for the material available on those Internet sites or on other Web sites they may link to. Any comments or suggestions can be sent by e-mail to comments@enslow.com or to the address on the back cover.

♻ Enslow Publishers, Inc., is committed to printing our books on recycled paper. The paper in every book contains 10% to 30% post-consumer waste (PCW). The cover board on the outside of each book contains 100% PCW. Our goal is to do our part to help young people and the environment, too!

Interior Photo Credits: © 1999 Artville, LLC, pp. 8–9. Dover Publications, Inc., pp. 5, 11, 19, 24, 32. Shutterstock.com: aleksandr hunta, p. 30; Balashova Ekaterina, p. 21 (background); BMJ, pp. 21 (snowy owl), 22 (lemming, snowy owl), 34, 37; Fexel, p. 38; Galyna Andrushko, p, 21 (flowers); gary yim, p. 7; Gertjan Hooijer, pp. 22 (musk oxen), 39; Gorillaimages, p. 29; Gouvi, pp. 22 (grasses, caribou), 28; Iakov Filimonov, p. 1; Incredible Arctic, pp. 10, 22 (saxifrage); Jean-Edouard Rozey, p. 22 (arctic fox); laceagatedesigns, pp. 16, 22 (landscape); Nadezhda Bolotina, p. 40; Pi-Lens, pp. 22 (lichen), 26; R. Vickers, p. 14; Sergey Uryadnikov, p. 4. © Thinkstock: Grigorii_Pisotckii/iStock, p. 15; hose_bw/iStock, pp. 17, 33; Incomel/iStock, p. 12; Jupiterimages/Photos.com, p. 35; MikeLane45/iStock, pp. 22 (jaeger), 41, 43; Murphy_Shewchuk/iStock, pp. 27, 31; photos_martYmage/iStock, pp. 21 (arctic hare), 22 (arctic hare), 36.

Cover Credits: HowardPerry/iStock/© Thinkstock (polar bears); owatta/Shutterstock.com (Earth illustration).

Dr. Jane Waterman is a biologist from the University of Central Florida. She studies the behavior of polar bears in Churchill, Manitoba, Canada, with her partner Dr. James Roth, also from the University of Central Florida. The volunteers depicted in Chapter 1 are from Earthwatch Institute, a nonprofit organization. Earthwatch supports field science and conservation through the participation of the public. See www.earthwatch.org for more information.

CONTENTS

Two polar bears test each other's strength.

Chapter 1

Learning the Bear Facts

Polar bears can stand ten feet tall. Two polar bears standing up and trying to push each other over can be a scary sight. Dr. Jane Waterman is filming two such bears from the safety of a tundra buggy. She is a scientist studying polar bear behavior near Manitoba, Canada. It is fall, and the air outside is crisp. The bushes on the low, rolling land are turning bright colors as far as the eye can see.

"See how they struggle with each other?" Dr. Waterman says,

pointing to the bears. "They are evenly matched. These are the same two that we watched yesterday."

The two bears are play-fighting. They stand on their back legs as if dancing together. They push each other and box with their giant paws. Sometimes they even bite. The bears will not hurt each other. They seem to be just testing each other's strength.

Canada's Polar Bears

Every summer, more than a thousand polar bears come south from the Arctic Ocean to the Churchill area in Canada. They spend the summer there, waiting for the ice to form again on the Arctic Ocean. When fall comes, some male polar bears gather and play-fight. They may do this for as long as an hour at a time. Polar bears are one of the few adult mammals to show this unusual behavior. Dr. Waterman wants to know why they play-fight.

"There's another advance from the one on the right," says Dr. Waterman. "And another, backing up the one on the left." She sounds like a sports announcer describing a boxing match.

Dr. Waterman continues filming the bears while a volunteer assistant takes notes. They keep track of how

Autumn on the tundra is a brightly colored, beautiful scene.

long the bears play-fight. They count the times each
bear tries to hit or push the other. Another volunteer
takes photographs to help identify each bear. When the
scientists get back to the lab, they watch the video and
take more notes. Every movement the bears make is
observed.

Learning About Polar Bears

Scientists like Dr. Waterman study play-fighting to
understand polar bears better. They wonder: How is play-

LEGEND

Tundra

Taiga

Temperate forest

Grassland

Desert

Rain forest

Chaparral

Mountain zone

Polar ice

Churchill, Manitoba

CANADA

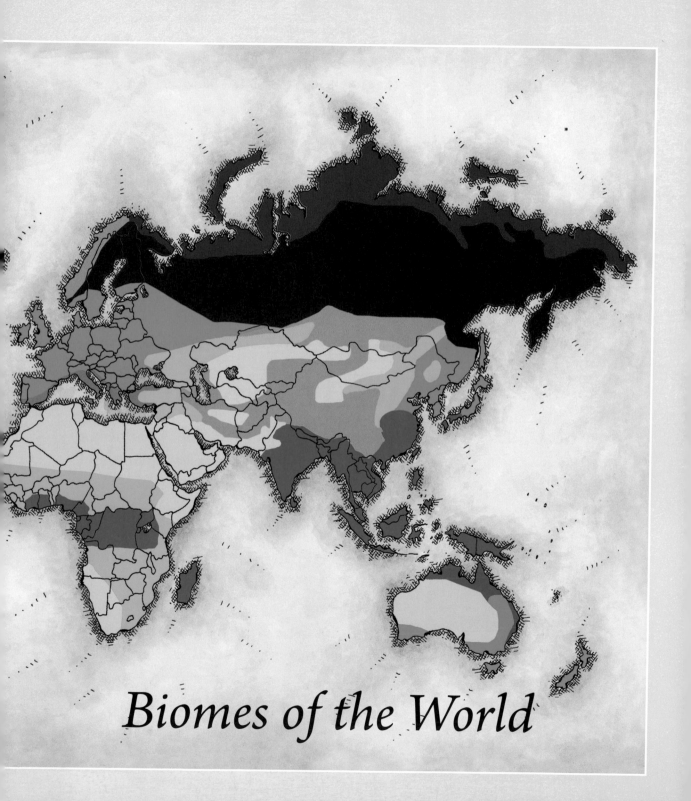

Biomes of the World

fighting important for the bears' survival? Are the bears just having fun, or does winning have some advantage? Are they practicing for real fights during the mating season?

Can the bears tell from play-fighting who is stronger? Can this help them avoid getting hurt later? Maybe the play-fighting simply helps get them in shape for the winter. The huge, open land where polar bears spend the summer is called tundra. It has many special plants and animals. Scientists try to understand how they live together in the tundra and how they affect each other's lives.

WHAT IS A BIOME?

The tundra is one kind of biome. A biome is a large region of Earth where certain plants and animals live. They survive there because they are well suited to the climate found in that area. The climate is a result of the temperatures and amounts of rainfall that usually occur during a year.

Each biome has plants that may not be found in other biomes. Trees grow in forests, but not in deserts. Cacti grow in deserts, but not in grasslands. The animals that eat these plants help form the living community of a biome.

Chapter 2

The Tundra Biome

Arctic tundra is found in the far northern part of the world. It is a land swept by frigid winds. (There is also alpine tundra, mountains around the world where it is too cold for trees to grow.) The arctic tundra is covered with ice and snow most of the year. One fifth of Earth's land is tundra, including parts of Canada, Alaska, Russia, Finland, Greenland, Iceland, Denmark, Sweden, and Norway.

The word *tundra* comes from the Finnish word *tunturia,*

The tundra is covered with low-growing plants. This field is in Alaska.

meaning "treeless plain." The land is covered with low-growing plants. There are no tall trees, and the only trees grow knee-high because of the harsh conditions.

Tundra Weather

Winters are long, lasting seven or eight months, and bitter cold. Winter temperatures average –30 degrees Fahrenheit (–35 degrees Celsius). Sometimes it gets as cold as –60 degrees Fahrenheit (–50 degrees Celsius). Because the tundra is so far north, it is dark through the long winter. The sun does not rise for several months. When it does, it is only for a short time.

On the other hand, there is daylight on the tundra for most of the summer. The sun does not set at night, or it sets for only a short time and is up again. But the tundra summer is short. The ground is still covered with snow in June, and snow starts to fall again by the middle of September. Temperatures rarely get above 50 degrees Fahrenheit (10 degrees Celsius). Plants and animals of the tundra have to grow and reproduce quickly during the short summer.

A Frozen Desert

It is so cold in the tundra that part of the ground is permanently frozen. In the summer, only the surface of the soil thaws. The layer of thawed soil is often only a couple of feet thick, and at most about five feet. Underneath this is a layer of soil that stays frozen all the time, called permafrost. Permafrost has a big effect on life in the tundra.

Permafrost is a layer of frozen ground below the surface soil.

During the long winter months, temperatures can dip as low as –60 degrees Fahrenheit. Notice the bird, called a willow ptarmigan, in its winter coloration. It blends in with the snow.

When the winter snow melts, much of the water is trapped on the surface. The solid permafrost below does not let the water drain away. As a result, many shallow lakes, marshes, and bogs form in the summer. Many plants and animals of the tundra live near these bodies of water.

The tundra is covered with snow in the winter and is full of wetlands in the summer. Still, it is a dry environment.

In the summer, shallow lakes form on the tundra. The water comes from melting snow.

It gets less than 10 inches (25 centimeters) of precipitation, or rain and snow, each year. That is about as dry as some deserts.

Most precipitation on the tundra is in the form of snow. Some drizzle and fog comes in the summer, too. The overall dryness of the tundra makes it a challenge for living things

TUNDRA FACTS

Extreme cold.

Low precipitation: Less than 10 inches (25 centimeters) of rain or snow fall each year, mostly as snow.

Permafrost: The short summer allows only the first 1 to 5 feet (0.3 to 1.5 meters) of soil to thaw. Beneath that is frozen soil, or permafrost.

Scarce nutrients: The frozen soil locks nutrients away where plants cannot get them.

Short growing season: Plants grow for less than three months.

Slow rate of decay: Soil animals and fungi that break down dead plants and animals move slowly in the cold.

to survive. And just as your hair dries faster on a breezy day, the howling wind makes the tundra environment drier still.

Rare Plant Food

The extreme cold of the tundra environment makes it difficult for plants to get nutrients. Nutrients are chemicals in the soil that plants need to live and grow. The layer of thawed soil into which the roots of plants can grow is thin. There are few nutrients for them to take in. Some nutrients are frozen in the permafrost. Other nutrients are held in the bodies of dead plants and animals.

Bacteria, insects, worms, fungi, and other living things work to break down dead plants and animals. But the bacteria work very slowly in the cold, wet soils. So there are few nutrients present for the plants.

Chapter 3

Biome Communities

Like every other biome, the tundra is made up of living communities of plants and animals. Communities are the groups of living things found together in a place. Within a community, some plants and animals depend on others. The plants and animals interact with each other every day. Each living thing has a role in the community.

Energy Flow in the Tundra

Plants in a community trap energy from sunlight for their food. They use the sun's energy to make sugar from carbon dioxide (a gas in the air) and the water from the soil. They later use the energy in the sugars to build new leaves, stems, roots, and flowers.

Some animals, such as caribou and arctic hares, eat these plants. Animals that eat only plants are called herbivores. Herbivores get their energy from plants. Other animals, called carnivores, eat herbivores. Arctic foxes and snowy owls are carnivores. Carnivores get their energy from eating the meat of other animals. Omnivores, such as birds called plovers, eat both plants and animals.

When plants and animals die, it is time for soil animals and fungi to get to work. They help break down the dead plants and animals. This releases nutrients back into the soil. Earthworms, beetles, fungi, microbes, and other soil life step in to do this job. These animals are called decomposers.

The Food Web

The flow of energy from the sun to plants to herbivores to carnivores follows a pattern called a food web. The food

SUNLIGHT

USED BY →

 **PLANTS** 〰 HEAT LOSS

EATEN BY →

 HERBIVORES 〰 HEAT LOSS

EATEN BY →

 **CARNIVORES** 〰 HEAT LOSS

SOIL LIFE breaks down plants and animals when they die.

At each stage in the energy flow through the tundra community, some energy is lost in the form of heat.

Some Plants and Animals in the
TUNDRA FOOD WEB

PLANTS	HERBIVORES	CARNIVORES
	Eaten by →	**Eaten by** →

PLANTS

Willows

Grasses

Lichens

Lupines

Saxifrage

HERBIVORES

Arctic Hares

Lemmings

Ptarmigans

Musk Oxen

Caribou

Ducks

Insects

CARNIVORES

Arctic Foxes

Snowy Owls

Jaegers

Wolves

Plovers

SOIL LIFE

Beetles   Worms   Bacteria   Fungi

web connects the plants and animals of a community, showing who eats whom.

Plants and animals use energy to live. They also pass this energy through the community. At each stage of the food web, some energy is lost as the animals use it to live. Plants must trap more energy from the sun to keep plants and animals in the community alive.

Learning From Biomes

Exploring biomes like the tundra is a good way to learn how living communities work. By looking at the plants and animals in any biome, you may see how some of them interact with each other. If you take any plant or animal away, it could change how the community works.

Chapter 4
Tundra Plants

The permafrost found in the tundra prevents the growth of tall trees. Tall trees need deep soil for deep root systems. But the tundra has only a shallow layer of soil over the permafrost. The only trees that can be found in the tundra are unlike the trees we know. They form a dense mat of woody growth close to the ground. The tallest things in the landscape are not trees, but rocks.

Arctic willow and dwarf birch trees are examples of these low-growing tundra trees. They might reach knee-high in spots where they are protected by snowdrifts in the winter. The snowdrifts shield them from the coldest temperatures and the harsh wind. The trees grow very slowly.

Not many kinds of plants can survive in the tundra. They cover the ground in low, thickly tangled mats with shallow roots. Herbs, grasses, and shrubs grow together with dense growths of lichens. Lichens look like small plants but are actually made of fungi and algae mixed together. They are very tough and thrive in the harsh tundra environment. A common one is reindeer lichen, or reindeer moss. The thick mat of lichens and plants is spongy and often wet. In the wettest places, sedges, such as cotton grass, are common.

The Shape of Tundra Plants

The tundra has the simplest structure of any biome. It has only one layer of plants growing low to the ground. All tundra plants have the greatest possible chance to gather sunlight because there are no tall trees to shade

Red lichens grow on a rock. Lichens are fungi and algae mixed together.

them. Still, they all grow very slowly because of the short, cool summers and the lack of nutrients.

The low tundra plants are protected from the cold and wind. They grow densely packed together. Cushion plants, which look like round couch cushions, form tight little mounds to shield themselves from the cold.

Many plants in the tundra have tiny hairs on their stems or dark leaves to help absorb the warmth from the sun. Others have small, leathery leaves to protect them from drying out. These and other special features help different plants survive the harsh tundra winter.

This tundra flower is covered with tiny hairs. The hairs help the plant absorb heat from the sun.

Herbs, grasses, and shrubs on the tundra grow in low clumps. They are packed tightly together.

The Tundra Year

Most tundra plants are perennials, meaning that they come back each summer from the same root. They store nutrients in their roots for the winter so they can get a head start on growth in the summer. Each summer the perennials continue their slow, steady growth and store more nutrients in their roots. Annuals, which are plants that grow from a new seed each year, are more delicate

A bee pollinates an anemone flower on the tundra.

Yellow poppies are one of the summer-blooming tundra plants. Their bright color attracts insects, which pollinate the flowers.

and take more energy to flower. They are not very common in the tundra.

The short tundra summers bloom with a burst of flowers. The low mat of plants becomes a rainbow of color. Blue lupines, pink saxifrage, white Labrador tea, and other flowers decorate the land. Their bright colors and sweet nectar attract insects that carry pollen from one blossom to another. This helps flowers make seeds for the next year's plants.

In autumn, many plants have nutritious berries, including cranberry, bilberry, crowberry, soapberry, and bearberry. Tundra animals eat these berries.

Plants of the tundra supply energy that flows through the tundra food web. They feed a variety of animals that changes with the seasons.

TUNDRA PLANTS

No tall trees: Only a few low-growing trees.

Many lichens and mosses.

Wind protection: Plants form a dense, tangled mat to protect themselves from cold and wind. Some form mounds or cushions for the same reason.

Fast flowering and fruiting in summer.

Shallow roots: Some tree roots reach only one foot deep.

Hairy stems and dark leaves help plants absorb more energy from the sun.

Mostly perennials.

Chapter 5

Tundra Animals

Using the energy and nutrients stored in tundra plants, tundra animals continue the food web of this biome. Yet very few animals can survive the long, dark tundra winter. There are many more animals in the tundra in the summer than in the winter.

Most birds migrate south to warmer places for the winter. Small animals, such as insects, seem to disappear for the winter. Insect eggs and pupae actually spend the winter waiting to become active in the summer. They are protected underground, under rocks, and under the bark of trees.

Reptiles and amphibians, like snakes and frogs, are not found in the tundra. They cannot keep themselves warm like birds and mammals can. They cannot fly and migrate south for the winter.

Those animals that do survive the tundra winter have special ways to deal with the cold and lack of food. They have very warm fur or feathers, and they are able to find just enough food to survive.

Surviving the Tundra Winter

Lemmings are small mammals that burrow under the snow. There, they feast on grasses, mosses, and twigs. They have a thick coat of fur and compact bodies to keep warm. Their small ears and short tail do not lose as much body heat as larger ones would. Heat leaves from the

The ground squirrel's fur helps it survive the tundra winter.

Lemmings eat grass, moss, and twigs beneath the tundra snow.

surface of the body. The less surface there is, the less heat loss there is.

Another advantage lemmings have is the ability to have many babies. They can have three litters of young in a year. Each litter may have ten babies, and these begin breeding when they are only weeks old. Their numbers can grow very quickly. Their population might continue to grow if it weren't for arctic foxes and other carnivores, such as snowy owls and birds called jaegers.

Arctic foxes are predators, which means they hunt other animals for food. They are very good at catching lemmings under the snow. Arctic foxes are also adapted to the tundra winter. They have a thick white winter coat that changes to brown in the summer. Their changing color helps them blend in with the land. The predator will not be as

An arctic fox leaps to pounce on its prey.

*An arctic hare in
its winter coat.*

noticeable to its prey if it blends in with the surroundings.
Arctic foxes are about the size of a large house cat. Like the
lemmings, they have compact bodies, short legs, and small
ears to help save their body heat.

Arctic hares also have thick fur that changes from white
to brown with the seasons. The hare's changing color helps
it blend into the land like the arctic fox. But in this case, it is
to hide from predators. Arctic hares have quite small ears
for a hare. Their feet, shaped like snowshoes, let them run

across the snow with ease. Arctic hares live in groups of as many as one hundred. Like lemmings, they have many babies.

One of the predators of arctic hares is the snowy owl, which also hunts for lemmings. Snowy owls are covered with fluffy white feathers from their beak to their talons. Their feathers keep in their body heat. Snowy owls can stay warm through most of the tundra winter. They migrate south only during very cold winters or when there are not many lemmings or hares to eat.

Other animals can be found in the tundra during the winter, but there are not many. Musk oxen are large, hoofed animals with long, shaggy fur. There are also ptarmigans, round chicken-like birds with a thick coat of feathers. Depending on the weather conditions, red foxes and wolves may wander

A snowy owl eats both arctic hares and lemmings. This predator has feathers to keep it warm.

onto the tundra during winter. These animals continue the flow of energy over the frozen tundra. Yet there is little energy on hand, and life is hard for those that survive. Nothing is wasted.

Summer in the Tundra

The tundra community is very different in the summer. Many animals come from the south to enjoy the endless daylight. They also find a feast of resources. Insects come out from their winter hiding and swarm to the shallow wetlands. They dine on the nectar of flowering plants and

The rock ptarmigan is another animal found on the tundra. It makes its nests in low tundra grass and shrubs.

A musk ox mother and calf stand in the tundra.

the blood of animals. Mosquitoes, deer flies, black flies, bumblebees, and moths are thick in the air.

Millions of migratory birds join in the feeding frenzy. They nest on the tundra during the short summer months. Sparrows, horned larks, longspurs, and buntings nest in the low tundra plants. Waterfowl, such as geese, ducks, and swans, and wading birds, such as plovers, phalaropes, and godwits, flock to the shallow lakes. Golden plovers come from as far as Argentina, in South America, 8,000 miles (about 13,000 kilometers) away.

In the summer, herds of caribou travel to the tundra.

Young birds grow very quickly on the feast of insects. The birds need to develop fast so that they are large enough to migrate south before winter. Tundra predators hunt these summer visitors. Especially in years when the number of lemmings is low, arctic foxes and other predators eat many of the birds' eggs and young.

Caribou are large deer that move onto the tundra in the summer. They come from forests to the south, where they find food and shelter in the winter. In the summer, they give birth to their calves and feed on the tundra's new plant growth. They move in giant herds of tens of thousands. Sometimes herds travel more than 1,000 miles (1,600 kilometers) in a year in search of the best food.

Caribou are followed onto the tundra by wolves, which prey on the newborn caribou calves. The wolves are social hunters. They live in packs and work together to stalk large prey. Like other predators,

Wading birds, such as the stilt sandpiper, have long legs. They arrive near the shallow tundra lakes to nest.

wolves continue the flow of energy on the tundra. Energy is collected from the sun by tundra plants. The plants are eaten by herbivores, such as caribou calves. Then the energy goes to the wolves and other carnivores.

Polar Bears in the Tundra

The polar bears studied by Dr. Jane Waterman come to the tundra for the summer also. Since female polar bears have babies on the tundra, their survival relies on the health of the tundra. They eat relatively little during their time on land, so they only take a little from the tundra food web. However, polar bears have been known to help themselves to lichens, berries, and grasses. They will even eat snow geese and lemmings on occasion.

The tundra is a delicate environment, one that can be affected by changes on our planet. For example, the rising temperature of our planet, called global warming, is having a serious effect on polar bears. With Earth getting warmer, the pack ice is breaking up earlier in the spring. As a result, polar bears are spending more time on land. Because they eat little while they are on land, polar bears can lose two pounds of weight each day. The more days they spend on land, the skinnier they get. Polar bears are at risk of starving.

The tundra is a unique place, filled with unique communities of life. The tundra plants and animals survive harsh winters and short summers. These plants and animals help form the tundra food web. Energy flows through them to make this frozen land one full of life.

ANIMAL FACTS

Fur or feathers keep in body heat.

Compact bodies lose less heat than long, skinny ones.

Small ears and tails lose less body heat than long ones.

Large feet help animals walk on top of the snow, like snowshoes.

Changing colors: Many animals change their coat color from white in winter to brown in summer to blend in with the land.

Many migratory birds fly from the south for the summer feast of insects and for the long daylight.

Rapid growth: Young animals must grow fast to be big enough to migrate south in the fall or to survive the winter.

Insects wait out the cold winter in the form of eggs or pupae. Their life cycle continues when insects emerge in the summer.

WORDS TO KNOW

ADAPTATION—A trait of a plant or animal that helps it live under certain conditions.

ANNUAL—A plant that lives for only one year. The following year, new members of the species grow from seeds.

BIOME—An area of the earth defined by the kinds of plants that live there.

BOG—An area of wet, spongy ground.

CARNIVORE—An animal that eats other animals.

CLIMATE—The average weather conditions in an area, usually measured over years. It includes temperature, precipitation, and wind speeds.

COMMUNITY—The collection of plants and animals living and interacting in an area.

CUSHION PLANTS—Plants that grow in tight mounds to protect themselves from the cold and wind.

DECAY—The breakdown of dead plants or animals into nutrients by bacteria, fungi, and other living things.

FOOD WEB—The connections between living things that allow the transfer of energy from the sun to plants to herbivores to carnivores to creatures of decay.

HERBIVORE—An animal that eats plants.

LICHEN—A plantlike life-form made of fungi and algae that help each other survive.

MICROBE—A very simple, very small organism made of a single cell. Microbes break down dead animals and plants. There are many kinds of microbes, and there are many millions of microbes in a spoonful of soil.

MIGRATE—To travel from one place to another on a regular seasonal schedule.

NUTRIENTS—Important chemicals, such as minerals, that plants and animals need to survive and grow.

PERENNIAL—A plant that stores nutrients in its roots in order to survive through the winter. The same plant blooms every year from the root rather than from a seed.

PERMAFROST—The deep layer of soil under the tundra that remains frozen all year.

POLLINATION—The transfer of pollen from one flower to another by wind or by insects such as bees and flies. Pollination is necessary for the flower to make seeds and reproduce.

PRECIPITATION—Water falling in a given area in the form of rain or snow.

PREDATOR—An animal that hunts other animals for food.

SEDGE—Grasslike plants that are most commonly found in marshes and bogs.

TALON—The claw of a bird of prey.

VEGETATION—The plants growing in an area.

WETLAND—Areas, such as swamps, that have a large amount of moisture in the soil.

LEARN MORE

Benoit, Peter. *Tundra.* New York: Scholastic, 2011.

Byles, Monica. *Life in the Polar Lands.* Princeton, N.J.: Two-Can Publishing, 2000.

Latham, Donna. *Tundra.* White River Junction, Vt.: Nomad Press, 2010.

Steele, Philip. *Tundra.* Minneapolis, Minn.: Carolrhoda Books, 1997.

Stonehouse, Bernard. *The Poles.* New York: Crabtree Publishing Company, 2001.

Walker, Tom. *Caribou: Wanderer of the Tundra.* Portland, Oreg.: Graphic Arts Center Publishing Company, 2000.

INDEX